Raspberry PI Beginners Guide:

The ultimate Raspberry PI 4 setup, programming, projects guide for beginners. Learn programming skills and become a master in computer technology

Ricardo C. Childress

Introduction

We are able to find a lot of different programming languages to work with to write codes and a lot of tools and accessories that sneak in and help us get things done as well. With all this technology growing and changing all the time, sometimes, this is going to make beginners feel like they are too far behind and that they should just give up rather than trying. They worry that the work is going to be too hard for them to get it done. The neat thing here is that Raspberry Pi is going to be there in order to help to solve this problem. This is going to be a small computer board, which is about the size of a credit card, that can hook up to the computer monitor or your TV. It is going to be smaller in size, but it will have a lot of power with it and can provide people of all ages and experience levels with ways to explore how the world of computers work, and can make it easier to learn how to work with a variety of programming languages, whether we are looking at the Python language C++, and Scratch. Compared to some of the other methods of learning to program out there, this one is going to be a lot easier to work with.

It is going to be easier than most of the other tools for programming out there, and it is going to provide us with a safe way to learn and practice our skills, even as a beginner.

To start here, the Raspberry Pi device is going to be anything that we would expect our traditional desktop computer to do, such as processing different voices, looking online, creating tables, doing gaming, playing videos in HD, and more. Even more than this, we will find that this device also comes with the ability to interact with the world outside as well. There have been a lot of different projects in a digital manner that can be made with this device. This can include homes with birds that have cameras on them, meteorological stations, and even detectors that parents are able to work with. As you can see, there is actually quite a bit that we need to know when it is time to work with Raspberry Pi, and you will be able to utilize it for a lot of the different projects that are out there.

We are going to look at some of the options that are out there for this device, and we will learn some of the coding that are necessary in order to get it started. It is such a simple device that we can work with, but it really does make the difference when it comes to how well we are able to learn about and work with computers and even how we are able to work through the process of learning new coding and programming language.

If you take a look at the structure of the Raspberry Pi, the first thing you'll notice is how small it is. The size of a Raspberry Pi is similar to that of a typical credit card. This small form-factor of the Raspberry Pi is itself a characteristic feature of the device, although it may not look entirely like a final product straight out of the box.

When compared to the modern PC motherboards, the Raspberry Pi is a computer that has been made available to the general consumer in an extremely small form-factor, low price tag, and functionality, which you would normally expect from a full-sized Personal Computer. Owing to such characteristics, the Raspberry Pi is suitable for a wide range of purposes. Browsing the internet, playing modest video games, interacting with popular social media channels, the perfect system to learn programming and coding, all the way to using the Raspberry Pi in innovative and creative projects building devices such as retro emulator in variety of forms and controlling and handling complex circuits. The Raspberry Pi does not have one specific use, in reality; it's the complete opposite; in the sense that the limitations of the Raspberry Pi are in actuality the limitations of one's imagination regarding the projects in which this device can be used.

Moreover, there's an entire Raspberry Pi community on the internet dedicated to helping out people in their queries regarding the device. Whether you bought your first Raspberry Pi and need help setting it up or if you're using a Raspberry Pi in a project, you will be surprised at how positively and quickly the community joins the discussion forums and give their suggestions and feedback to your questions.

The Raspberry Pi is a computational device based on single-board architecture. The single-board architecture is a design scheme for computers in which the entire system is situated on a single circuit board. Just as how the Raspberry Pi is based on the single-board architecture, it has also inherited the small form-factor of the design, which is similar to the dimensions of a credit card. However, it is important to keep the power and functionality of a computer separate from the size of its motherboard or circuit, because such parameters of a system are not dependent on how big of a circuit the system is situated upon. As such, the Raspberry Pi is capable of handling and performing all the tasks a Personal Computer would be able to do, but the speed at which the tasks are performed is another realm of the discussion by factoring in different parameters.

The birth of Raspberry Pi was inspired by the notion that fully functioning computers in a compact size made available to the general consumer at a plausible price would hold enough power as to not only facilitate the educational industry but also making computer technology easy to implement and customize in various projects (educational projects, DIY projects or any experiment that can use the prowess of the Raspberry Pi); in short, the prospects are virtually unlimited). The Raspberry Pi Foundations was established in 2012, and after a limited production of units, the beta testing became a huge success and today, Raspberry Pi is the leading device which has taken a strong foothold in various human interactive environments including homes, offices, smart factories, data centers, interactive classrooms and other such places which can take advantage of the features of a small hand-held computer.

Raspberry Pi Tour

Raspberry Pi 3

The last model before the fourth iteration, the Raspberry Pi 3, came with a newer processor at the time: the Broadcom BCM 2837. Being the 64-bit processor, not 32-bit, the new processor was considerably faster than the BCM 2836 found in the Raspberry Pi 2 version, which at the time was a massive upgrade from the BCM 2835 of the original and the Plus series. The Raspberry Pi 3 was also the first model to get built-in wireless support, which included a radio that connected to 2.4 GHz Wi-Fi networks and Bluetooth devices.

One great advantage of the new Pi 3, other than the built-in wireless features and of course, the improved performance is its 64-bit processor. Switching over to this model given its new processor means that you will have better software compatibility performance and security over the 32-bit version of the older models.

Raspberry Pi 3 Model B

This model is a further improvement of the B model board. It has the same dimensions, but the quad-core processor comes with a 1.2 GHz chip. This Raspberry Pi version is also the first one to feature a wireless connection and onboard Bluetooth without requiring any external devices to be connected.

Raspberry Pi 4

The Raspberry Pi 4 Model B

One of the most critical components is the system-on-chip (SoC), which is the centerpiece covered in a metal cap, as shown in the image above.

It is called system-on-chip as there is a silicon chip underneath the metal cover if you pry it open. This chip is also known as an integrated circuit that contains most of the Raspberry Pi's operating system. Some of the most critical aspects contained within the chip are the graphics processing unit (GPU), handles the visual side of things, and the central processing unit (CPU), also known as the brain of a computer.

But without memory, the CPU would be of no use. But if you were to look to the side of the SoC, you'll find another small, black, plastic square chip (as the image shows), which is the board's random-access memory (RAM). This RAM, when in use, holds whatever you're doing and will write it to the microSD card when you save your work. To reiterate from what we said earlier, the RAM is volatile, which means when the Pi board is powered off, you lose your data. On the other hand, the microSD card is non-volatile, and if you save your data in it, you won't be able to lose it even when the power is out.

Then at the top left a corner of the board, you'll come across another silver lid which covers the radio, which is what gives the Raspberry Pi its ability to connect with other devices wirelessly. The radio behaves as two separate components: a Wi-Fi radio that wirelessly connects to other computer networks; and the Bluetooth radio that connects to peripherals like keyboards and mice or for sending or receiving data from nearby smart devices such as sensors or smartphones.

Then there's the USB controller represented by a black, plastic-covered chip that's at the bottom edge of the board just behind the middle set of USB ports.

More on Differences

CPU: The Raspberry Pi 4 runs on 1.5GHz CPU: The Raspberry Pi 3 runs on 1.4 GHz Video Out: Raspberry Pi 4 has dual micro HDMI ports

Video Out: Raspberry Pi 3 has a single HDMI port

Power requirement: Raspberry Pi 4 has 3A and 5V

Power requirement: Raspberry Pi 3 has 2.5A and 5V

Raspberry Pi design

As outlined earlier, the Raspberry Pi 4 size is 3.5 x 2.3 x 0.76 inches (88 x 58 x 19.5 mm) and also 0.1 pounds (46 grams), which makes it possible for it to enter your pocket and it is also light in weight to be carried to all places.

The Raspberry Pi 4 board is durable to make it stay in your bad; however, you should stick it in a thing which can protect and guide it, especially to safeguard the pins. Meanwhile, while testing the board and Pi 4, the board bare is always on the table, and it is moved front and back between my place of work and office alike as it places it in a cardboard box that has no static or padding bag.

The older models of the Raspberry Pi have a single, full-size HDMI port, the double micro HDMI connectors found on the Raspberry Pi 4 do not interfere with the Pi 3 model. There is a case that costs $10 and 8.50 in Euros, and it is known as Pimoroni Pibow. It is known to be very good, but the fault with it is that it does not cover the GPIO pins.

The Raspberry Pi 4 is known to cover a lot when the ports come into question.

The Raspberry Pi 4 right-hand side has four USB Type-A connections, two of the four USB Type-A connections are USB 3.0. Also, there is a full-size Gigabit Ethernet port that serves as a wired connection. The lower edge of the Raspberry Pi 4 has a 3.5 mm audio jack, USB Type C charging port as well as two micro HDMI ports. On the left-hand side of the Raspberry Pi 4 is a micro SD card reader.

On the top surface of the Raspberry Pi board is, you will be able to view the ribbon connectors for the Camera Serial Interface (CSI) as well as a Display Serial Interface (DSI) which provides for connections to Raspberry Pi's screen, camera, and compatible accessories.

Storage performance It does not matter how the rate at which your processor, GPU, and RAM run if you possess slow storage, you will find it very difficult if you want to open your applications and files alike.

All Raspberry Pi, the micro SD card reader, is the Pi 4 storage device, which makes for its convenience but somewhat restricted.

The Raspberry Pi Foundation made it clear that Pi 4 has a high transfer rate of 50 Mbps, which is two times the speed of the card reader on Pi 3. There is no certain limit on the capacity of Pi 4.

Some experiments were done with a Samsung EVO Plus micro SD XC class 10 card, which displayed fewer rates than the maximum. The Pi 4 read and write the rates, which includes 45.7 and 27.7 Mbps, respectively. The Pi 3 was left behind to read and write 22.8 and 17.5 Mbps respectively.

Users that have an external SSD or a fast USB flash drive, you will experience a much better storage performance on your Raspberry Pi 4. The Pi 4 has a whopping 3 USB ports which have a high bandwidth of 625 Mbps.

While making use of a Western Digital Blue SSD in a USB to M.2 enclosure, it was seen that the speed of transfer was recorded as 2 to 13 x faster than the original micro SD card. Also, the applications which were slow in responding and opening began to open much quicker with the SSD that was attached. Sadly, a normal USB flash drive is slower than the micro SD card.

You should be aware that currently, the Raspberry Pi 4 firmware does not permit one to boot off an external drive. The solution you will have to take is run all of your programs, which includes most of the OS.

However, note that there would be a firmware update in the coming months that will fix this issue. Quick USB 3 ports are much more and serve the function than just storage. The likes of Google's Coral USB Accelerator, which assists in artificial intelligence tasks, can be used.

Network performance

The new model of the Raspberry Pi has a similar 802.11ac Wi-Fi as its former model (Pi 3). However, it has Bluetooth 5.0, which is more improved than its predecessor.

Also, the Ethernet port has much more bandwidth, which permits it to give out a full gigabit. When the Ethernet port of the Raspberry Pi 4 was tested, it arrived at 943 Mbps, which is much greater than other models of Raspberry Pi. Extensive research done showed that the Pi 4 achieved 943 Mbps while its closest competitor arrived at just 237 Mbps. Since Raspberry Pi 4 and Pi 3 has the same 802.11ac Wi-Fi, which can run on 2.4 GHz bands, there is not much difference in performance.

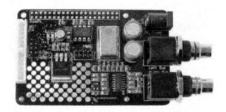

Audio phones plugged to Pi 3

Power and heat

The Pi 4 model is known to consume more power than the former models because it has a more power-hungry processor. When the Raspberry Pi 4 is idle, it collects about 3.4 watts, which is about 17% more than the former Pi 3.

Meanwhile, when the Raspberry Pi 4 is under load and active, it rises to 7.6 watts. Meanwhile, it is still a little 19% better than the Pi 3.

Users of Pi that need a lower power Pi, the Pi Zero W, is the best for you as it consumes only a small 0.8 watts when it is idle and 1.66 when it is active and under load.

The board in Pi 4 is much warmer than the former models. The areas of the Pi 4 board close to the CPU is often warm, not only the top of the processor that gets warm. The Raspberry Pi 4 has up to 74.5 degrees Celsius, which is not enough for it to heat up and possibly burn. While Pi 3 has up to 62.5 degrees Celsius, which is lower than the new model.

A CPU intensive workload was tested for 10 minutes, and it was seen that the processor got to 81 degrees and started to go down from 1.5 to 1 GHz after a couple of minutes. Meanwhile, the processor began to regain itself to 1.5 GHz when it came down to 80 degrees.

GPIO pins

The new model pins support four extra 12C, SPI as well as UART connections.

You can get a much quicker response and speed with the GPIO pins on the Raspberry Pi 4 because of its faster processor.

Web surfing. The web surfing you get on the Pi 4 is much better than you will get with other models because of its faster processor. The Pi 4 runs on 4GB RAM as compared with other older models, which makes surfing the web faster and enjoyable.

Web hosting

You can open heavy pages and serve guests simultaneously because it gives 3983 requests per second than 2850 that the Raspberry Pi 3 gives. A lot of web apps make use of the PHP server-side scripting language. That means a much faster and quicker processor can assist the PHP in some way. You can get the best of hosting web pages on your Pi 4 and other older models.

Compiling code

Having Linux, in some cases, you will have to compile programs you wish to install. A lot of instances, when testing is done, there is a need to compile software packages so that an object recognition demo can start.

For the Raspberry Pi 4 to compile code quicker, a faster processor and much better RAM is needed, and it is efficient in Pi 4 than other older versions.

Raspberry PiAccessories and Uses

Micro-SD Card

In addition to the Raspberry Pi you need a Micro SD card. I recommend a 32 Gigabyte SD card for enough storage capacity. This is also available at Amazon.

Very important is, when you buy an SD card, pay attention to the classification. The card mentioned above has the class 10, which is necessary to ensure a reliable reading and writing speed. So be sure to check it if you buy another card than my recommendation.

Sensors and Modules

Another very useful extension is the sensor package from SunFounder. It contains 37 sensors for different applications. It contains numerous extensions for the Raspberry Pi, for example a remote control or a small LCD display. But there are also sensors of all kinds, including a plug-in board and cable connections. You can use it to carry out a whole host of experiments and projects. Link to the 37 Sensors Starter Kit from SunFounder.

Official Raspberry Pi power supply

A very important topic, which you should not neglect, is the power supply for the Raspberry Pi. Theoretically, you can connect any Micro-USB charger cable to the Raspberry Pi. However, the Raspberry Pi only tolerates a certain voltage, or must have a certain voltage, in order to function at all.

Otherwise you will get a permanent "Undervoltage Error Message" on your screen. This indicates that the power supply is too low. The Raspberry Pi cannot run at all or only with a limited CPU clock.

Raspberry Pi 3B+ Starter Kit

So far the overview of the Raspberry Pi accessories and where you can buy a Raspberry Pi. In general, of course, there are many Raspberry Pi starter packs, where you can find all sorts of accessories.

Raspberry Pis have a multitude of uses, some of which are more obvious than others are. Because they offer so much in terms of hardware compatibility relative to their small size, they have become the favorite of tinkerers. This makes them an obvious candidate for projects involving complex robotics.

Gaming Platforms

Perhaps the first thing that really tipped hobbyists off to how neat the Raspberry Pi was video games. Go figure, I suppose. Many people really like video games, and the Raspberry Pi is powerful and cheap enough that you can very easily build a dedicated emulator absolutely packed with games. The more powerful versions of the Raspberry Pi can even play Nintendo 64 games, which is incredible for how small of a computer it really is and how cheap it is.

While more resource-intensive games do stretch its capabilities, it does find a safe home being able to play a multitude of classic NES and SNES games, as well as games for other consoles like the Sega Genesis, the Amiga, and so on. The first hobbyist implementations of the Raspberry Pi were often in dedicated gaming stations as such.

One popular implementation for the Pi was handheld gaming consoles. These would be things like a portable Super Nintendo and NES that only really had to be about the size of the Raspberry Pi itself. If you affix an LCD or LED screen to the Raspberry Pi and solder some buttons onto it, you would have a super cool portable gaming console with a rechargeable battery. These aren't terribly popular anymore, largely because the battery life wasn't that great and the novelty wore off, but they still are an exciting first project to undertake.

Speaking of video games, many people will actually use the Raspberry Pi as a MAME emulator. MAME emulators are emulators built to run arcade games like those you would find at a classic arcade.

Magic Mirror

I think my personal favorite implementation of the Raspberry Pi would be the Magic Mirror. The Magic Mirror is what it sounds like: it's a mirror with a digital display like the ones you would see in old sci-fi shows. All of the information you need is right at your fingertips, and some people have even programmed in voice recognition to these things so that they can control them with their voice. Using motion detectors or light sensors, the mirror would be able to detect when you're around and power on automatically, or it may be always on. It's not a huge power draw, after all—the same as constantly having an alarm clock plugged in.

I'm going to spend a second talking about this because I think it's super cool and ingenious. The magic mirror is one of my favorite implementations of Raspberry Pi bar none because of the amount of creativity and ingenuity that goes into it. It's cheap to make (comparatively), and you can actually make an amazing machine out of it—not to mention that there's nothing else like it. There is no mass-marketed magic mirror. You will be one of the only people with this and you made it yourself, too!

So let's think about the magic mirror for a second. What happens is that there is a frame. Behind that frame sits a computer monitor, and behind that sits the Raspberry Pi. In front of the computer monitor (or TV, but usually a computer monitor) sits a one-sided mirror.

Because of the way the mirror reflects light, any black from behind the mirror won't be shown. However, any bright things that are directly up against the mirror will shine through. As I said, it's an ingenious implementation that really doesn't get enough credit. The Raspberry Pi will be set up to automatically run a full-screen Chromium browser with a custom web page. Other times, the webpage is just opened in a modified Webkit browser that automatically takes up the whole screen, like Chrome OS somewhat. Either way, the Raspberry Pi natively launches into this mode, and from here, we start to develop somewhat of an idea of how the thing should work overall.

The customized home page is a black background with white text and images, and this usually has some sort of complex JavaScript code powering it to make it truly customized. One way or another, though, the person ends up with a cool mirror. The mirror displays stuff like a "Good morning" or "Good evening" message, some have even been programmed to give a different compliment each day. Some will display stuff for the day like the weather or the latest news, and so on and so forth.

Raspberry Pi, because it is cost-efficient and relatively powerful, has also been used in various robotics projects. Raspberry Pi, as a result, has taken up some of the more complex artificial intelligence robotics projects that tinkerers want to take up, and other things similar.

Other Uses

Some people get seriously creative with the Raspberry Pi and will use it as the core of their media center. The Pi is great for this because it's low profile and has the capacity to store a huge amount of information in its small form-factor via its MicroSD slot. More than that, its internet connectivity also means it integrates seamlessly with services such as Spotify and Netflix.

Because of this, many people such as cinephiles and audiophiles will use the Raspberry Pi as a means from which to store and direct their home theater. Several infrastructures like Kodi catered specifically towards this and have been introduced over time and come to play a major part in the overall Raspberry Pi community.

The Bluetooth capabilities of the Raspberry Pi also mean that it's been opened up to use as a media center, speaker, and much more. Many people also take advantage of its WiFi compatibility and choose instead of using it as a whole media center to simplify and use it just as a place to stream stuff throughout the house. There are projects that actually link Raspberry Pis up to a central hub on the WiFi connection and then use this as a means to play music throughout the entire house, which is a seriously cool usage.

The Raspberry Pi also comes with built-in support for a ton of different sensors, thermostats, and things of the like. This means many people are using them to build things like robots that can automatically water their plants for them by detecting when they start to release excess amounts of carbon, or even stuff like automatically detecting what nutrients the plant is short on and could use more of.

Some people opt to buy multiple Raspberry Pis and use them in order to build a server farm. These server farms consist of interlinked Raspberry Pis on a central hub that accepts and distributes incoming traffic. Network junkies love Raspberry Pis for this reason. A simpler use would be to set up your own dedicated game server using a singular Raspberry Pi.

In the same vein, some people will buy multiple Raspberry Pis in an attempt to build a massive Bitcoin or cryptocurrency mining rig. While this has lost a lot of its efficiency for Bitcoin specifically because Bitcoin now needs an extremely strong processor and essentially a GPU farm in order to mine anything meaningful, newer cryptocurrencies—especially memory-hard cryptocurrencies—can be easily mined using Pi-based mining operations. While there are better investments if you're serious about starting a mining farm (such as a lot of GPUs), if you just have extra Raspberry Pis lying around from past projects, then it could be a really cool way to make use of them and try it out for yourself.

The Internet of Things

The Internet of Things is more the idea that your alarm goes off at 7, you press the snooze button 3 times, and when you finally get up and turn off the alarm properly, a signal is sent to your coffee maker and your TV. It starts automatically brewing coffee and turns on the TV so that you can watch the news that morning. This sort of thing is the basic idea behind the internet of things.

So how does Raspberry Pi fall into this equation? I'd say that in one way or another, it's actually self-explanatory. The Raspberry Pi is a beautiful way of providing a relatively powerful computer interface to everyday things. If you have a decent knowledge of electrical engineering, you could solder things, alter relays, and actually program your everyday appliances to work in this manner.

If you lack that sort of background knowledge, then you still have more than enough opportunities to build everything from the ground up, or even just use your Raspberry Pi as a hub that your entire Internet-based items can connect to, as more Internet-based items come out. Many people have already programmed things like automatic settings to their coffee makers or the aforementioned robots that would do things like automatically water plants or detect nutrient deficiencies. These sorts of things give you a clear idea of the possible uses of the Raspberry Pi in the context of the Internet of Things.

A great example of that rests in the fact that some people have taken up the task of using open-source voice recognition software in order to try to build their own version of things like Amazon Alexa. These projects show how capable the Raspberry Pi is of being used for various artificial intelligence applications.

Speaking of Amazon Alexa, many Raspberry Pi projects will interface with things such as Amazon Alexa or other home assistants in order to make voice-activated Pi commands a reality, among many other things.

There is, in the end, a plethora of different uses for the Raspberry Pi. There are even more than I've mentioned here. Really, in the end, the Raspberry Pi is a small and cost-effective computer.

Setup Guide

Now let's move on the steps to set up the system for you. You need to read the instructions carefully and move ahead properly so that everything is set up correctly.

If you have got the official case, then start by splitting it into five pieces. The five pieces will include the following things

- Red Base

- 2 white

- Sides

- Red upper

- White lid

1. Once you have ensured that you have got everything, use the base and hold it in such a way that the raised end is on the left side while the other on the right.

2. Now pick up the Raspberry Pi with the help of the USB and the Ethernet ports, but make sure that the GPIO header is on the top and the slot is on the left side. Once the position is according to the image shown now lower down the right side in the case so that it sits down in the case.

3. Now grab the two white sides and locate the one that provides the cut-outs for the power source, HDMI port, and 3.5 mm AV jack. Arrange it

accordingly, with the ports on the Raspberry Pi and push it into the case gently. Once you hear a click sound, you are sure of the fact that it will fit in.

4. Use the solid white part and insert into the GPIO header part of the case

5. Now use the red plastic upper piece and inset the clips on the left on to the matching holes that are available on the left-hand side of the case. This position is right above the microSD slot. Once the left side is in its proper position, it's time to push the right side (right above the USB ports) down until you hear a click.

6. Most of your system is set up, and now you will be moving on the final steps. Grab the white lid in such a way that the Raspberry Pi logo is to your right, and the minor raised clips on its bottom are creased up with the hole on the top of the case. Now push the board into the case until you hear a click.

Now your case is ready to be used for software setup which we will discuss next. Before you move on to the software, make sure that you have attached power supply, a monitor through the HDMI, a keyboard, mouse, and a microSD card to it.

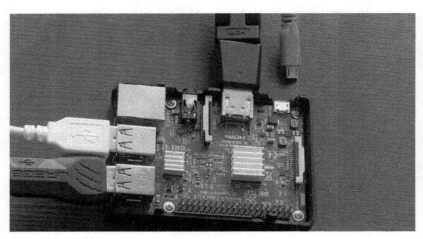

Raspbian OS for Raspberry Pi 3 and Pi 4

Once the hardware is set up, you need to move forward with the software setup so that you can use the system for whatever purposes you desire. The operating system is the main software that is required to be installed before you start working on your Raspberry Pi. In this book we will be installing NOOBS, the New Out-Of-Box Software that is specially designed to ensure that you get an exceptional experience. The setup will allow you to install from different options automatically.

At the initial startup, when the computer is booted it will show a plain screen with a Raspberry Pi logo on it and a minor window at the upper left corner of the screen. After waiting for a while, you will be shown the following screen as shown below:

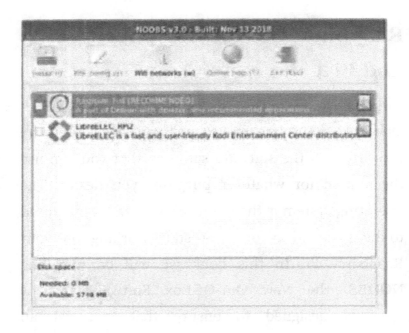

The above image shows you the NOBOS menu, which is a system that allows you to select from a list of the operating system that you wish to install on your system. Initially, only two operating systems are available for installation. The first one is the "Raspbian, a version of the Debian Linux operating system" that has been specially personalized for Raspberry Pi computers. The other one is the LibreELEC which was introduced by Kodi Entertainment Centre software.

To start off, you need to ensure that Pi is connected to the network; it could be connected through a wire or a Wi-Fi network. You can connect the computer from the top bar of icons available on the interface. *The interface also allows you the option of downloading and installing other operating systems.*

Now click the option with the left click, and you are good to go.

Once you are done with this step you will see "Install (i)" menu icon that will be enabled this time. *The enabling of this button tells you that the operating system is ready to be installed on your machine.*

Once the button is enabled, click it to begin the installation, before moving ahead, it will warn you that any data stored in the microSD will be overwritten excluding NOBOS. To proceed the installation, you click "Yes" and the installation process will begin. *This process can take up to 30-40 minutes depending upon the space and the speed of your microSD card. As the operating system is being installed you will see a progress bar on the screen that will tell the status of installation. As the installation progress, you will also see the list of features under the progress bar that is being installed.*

Warning:

There are a few things that need to be kept in mind while installing the Operating System on the computer. It is significant to ensure the fact that the installation is not interrupted as there is a high chance of the software getting corrupt. Moreover, also ensure that you do not remove microSD or unplug the power cable during the installation as this may corrupt the operating system.

If something like this happens, you need to unplug the pi from the power supply and then press the SHIFT key on the keyboard during this time you can connect back the Pi to the power supply.

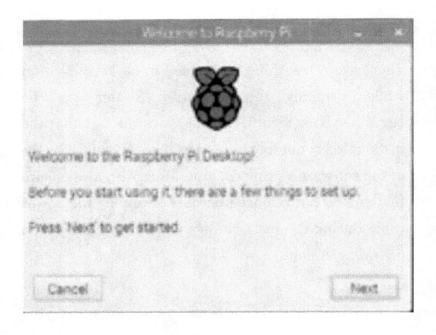

This will bring the NOBOS menu back on the restart. This step is known as the **recovery mode**, and it provides you an easy way to restore your computer in case of any mishap. It also gives you the option of entering into NOBOs menu after successful installation you can reinstall the OS, and you can even install any other OS you want.

Setting Up the Computer

Step 1.

Once the installation is done, a popup window will appear that will indicate that the installation is complete. After successful installation, the computer will restart, and you will see lots of messages on the command prompt as the first time it starts, it takes a few minutes to adjust itself.

Step 2.

Once everything is done, and the OS is sure that the user can use the system, the following popup will show up letting you know that you are good to go.

Step 3.

Now click next to proceed where you will be asked to set up Country, Language, and Time zone for the system.

Step 4.

One everything is filled hit Next to proceed to set up your password.

Step 5.

After you have set up your password, you need to set up a connection to the internet. You can do this by connecting your computer to your Wi-Fi network available in the given list. Just click the network you wish to connect and provide the password for the network to proceed.

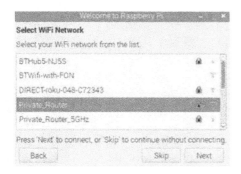

Step 6.

After adding a network connection to your computer hit next where you will be asked to ensure that the Raspberry Pi regularly checks for updates. These updates are introduced to fix bugs and bring new features and enhance performance capacities. If the window shows updates, then you need to be patient as updates might take a bit of time.

Step 7.

After installing the updates, the OS will ask you to reboot the system so that it can apply all the changes that you have made. Just hit the Reboot button and set aside to let the system reboot.

Recommended Software for Smooth Experience. The operating system comes along with some of the basic features that allow you to operate the computer with ease. Some of this software include

- **Chromium Browser**: It is a browser that will enable you to access different sites on the internet. It is a built-in tool for the Raspbian OS. If you have used chrome on any other machine, then you will be good to go as it is no different from it.

- **The File Manager**: It provides you the ability to manage your files on your brand-new Raspberry Pi. All your files are saved in your home directory by default. File manager allows the opportunity to browse the files and folders that are also regarded as directories. These files are located on your Micro SD card installed on your system. Your Raspberry Pi also allows you to attach removable storage media such as USB flash drives. Here are some directories that are created by default which help to arrange your documents according to their categories.

- Desktop

- Documents

- Downloads

- Music

- Pictures

- Public

- Videos

You will have a similar experience just as you have in Windows with these default folders on the left and all your files arranged on the right. Moreover, you can also copy all the files from the Raspberry Pi to your microSD attached to the computer. You can do this simply by copy-paste technique just as you do in Windows or any other Operating system.

- The LibreOffice: It is a collection of software that allows you to do specific tasks such as you can use the LibreOffice Word to type documents, manage or update them. Other software that is part of this suite are listed as follows:

- LibreOffice Base: It is a database tool for analyzing, arranging, and storing information.

- LibreOffice Calc: It is spreadsheet software that provides users the ability to manipulate with number and represent them through graphs.

- LibreOffice Draw: It is an illustration software that enables you to enhance your creative skills.

- LibreOffice Impress: It is a software that is designed to allow you to create slide shows.

- LibreOffice Math: It is a formula editor that provides formatted mathematical tools which could be easily used in other places.

Despite the fact that Raspbian comes along with numerous preloaded software, there is various other software which is compatible with it even more. As a user of Raspbian, you can pick and choose software available from the list. Raspbian is compatible with various software, and this software is hand-picked by the Raspberry Pi Foundation. This software is also available in the list of Recommended Software tool.

It is important to note that to install this recommended software, you will need a connection to the internet. Check the list of recommended software and click on the raspberry menu icon and go to

Preferences and then hit the option "Recommended Software." It will take a bit of time and will provide you a list of available software.

Raspberry Pi and Python

Python language presents a high-level syntax; we say this because its form of writing is very close to human language. Also, Python supports object-orientation.

Fundamentally, python requires precise writing of code, but it also offers a friendly user interface where you are guided along the way of writing codes by the application itself (marking mistakes in code and offering useful suggestions).

This specific integrated development environment for python has two modes, a normal mode and a Simple mode. The simple mode makes things even easier for beginners, and in this guide, we will be referring to the Simple model of this application.

A. This is the toolbar that you'll see while in the application's Simple Mode. Beneath each friendly icon on the toolbar, you'll see that they are labeled with the purpose for which they are used.

B. This is the application's script area. The purpose of this area is exactly similar to the Scratch application. We write down codes in this area, the numbering on the left side of this area indicates the line number. As you keep writing codes, it's automatically indexed. In the scenario where your code encounters an error, you will know which line of code the error is referring to and because every line is indexed, you can quickly navigate to the faulty line of code and fix it. This simple indexing can be useful and timesaving.

C. This is the Python Shell. This area provides information about the code which is currently being run by the application and, you can input individual lines of code and execute them by simply pressing the ENTER button.

D. This is specifically the variables area. This area shows you information (name and value) of all the variables that you created for a specific program.

Programming with Python: Making a Program

After you start up python, the first thing you will notice is that, unlike Scratch, there are no colorful blocks or sprites. This is because Python is more of a traditional programming language that relies on code being manually written down (without any typos or errors, of course!).

Open up python from the Raspberry Pi menu and wait for Thonny Python IDE to load up (Thonny will start-up in the Simple Mode by default). Go over to the Python shell area and type in

Print("Good Morning!")

After typing in the following instruction, all you need to do is press the ENTER key, and you'll see the message "Good Morning" displayed below the instruction. We have just created our first program. It was as simple as that!

As soon as you hit ENTER, the code will execute. On the other hand, when you press ENTER after writing a line of code, instead of executing the lines of code, you just get a new blank line to write more code. To execute the codes in the scripts area, you need to do so by clicking the 'Run' icon in the toolbar (When you click the Run button, Thonny will prompt you to save your current program first, just type in a name for your program and click save). Notice that when you run a saved program from the scripts area, the message in the shell area is a bit different this time

>>> %Run 'Name you used to save the program.py.'

Good Morning!

You can also write the same line of code in the scripts area as well, but this time, we'll use a different and more popular phrase "Hello, World!" and while saving it, we will give it the name Hello, World!
(Here's the message you'll see in the shell area)

>>> %Run 'Hello World.py'

Hello, World!

The First line basically instructs the Interpreter to execute the program, which has just been saved, and the second line is the end result or the output of running that program, in our case, displaying a message. We have successfully written our first program on Python and ran it in both interactive and script modes.

Using Loops and Code Indentation

Indentation is basically python's way of controlling the sequence in which the lines of code are executed. In Scratch programming, we would use the colorful blocks and place them above each other in the sequence, which we wanted, but in Python, we need to use indentation to tell the computer that this is the sequence in which the lines of code are to be run.

Open a new project by clicking on the 'New' icon in the toolbar. This will open a separate new window for you to work on. In the scripts area, type in the following lines of code;

```
print("Loop starting!")
for i in range (10):
```

In the above lines of code, the first line works exactly in the same way as demonstrated in the Print("Good Morning") example. However, the second line is rather interesting. This line actually initiates a definite loop sequence, with the defined limit being set by the range followed by the desired integer. The i is the loop counter which will count the number of times the program loops, in this case, it will count upwards till nine because the stop instruction is the number 10, as soon as the 9th loop is completed, the loop will exit. Also, look at the colon ":" at the end of the line. This tells the computer that the following lines of code are actually a part of the loop.

Moreover, in Scratch, we saw that the instruction which is to be added into the loop function could be placed on the loop block directly. But in Python, we indent the instruction code by using a colon (":"). An indentation is characterized by four blank spaces left at the beginning of the new line; the IDE application does this automatically as soon as you press ENTER after an indentation.

```
print("Loop starting!")
for i in range (10):
print("Loop number", i)
```

This indentation is what allows python to differentiate between instructions that are not included in the loop and instructions, which are to be included in the loop (this indented code is known as being nested).

All the lines following this indentation will automatically contain four blank spaces because Thonny assumes that the following lines of code will also be the part of the loop. This will keep happening until you have written all the instructions which are part of the loop. To close the indentation, simply make a new indented blank line and press BACKSPACE, this will return the line back to normal. Now, close the indentation as described and write the following line of code

print("Loop finished!")

The sequence of the lines of code should be something like this;

print("Loop starting!")

for i in range (10):

print("Loop number", i)

print("Loop finished!")

In this program, the first line and last line is outside of the loop because they are not indented. The second line is where the loop starts and contains the indentation, whereas the third line is part of the loop. Let's save this program as "indentation" and run the program. In the shell area, we will see the following output;

Loop starting!

Loop number 0

Loop number 1

Loop number 2

Loop number 3

Loop number 4

Loop number 5

Loop number 6

Loop number 7

Loop number 8

Loop number 9

Loop finished!

The reason why Python counts from zero instead of one is that Python is designed as a zero-indexed language. This means that it considers 0 as the beginning integer rather than 1. You can change this behavior by specifying the range instruction to be a range (1, 11) instead of range(10). With this, the loop will start counting from 1 to 10. You can do this for any number you want.

Just as how we used definite and indefinite loops in Scratch, the same can be done in Python. To use indefinite loops (loops that run forever), all you need to do is edit the 2nd line of code in the above program.

```
print("Loop starting!")
```

While True:

```
print("Loop running!")
```

```
print("Loop finished!")
```

You have now created an indefinite loop. This is because the end condition of the loop has not been specified as each time the message "loop running!" is printed, the program directs the code execution back to the start, and the whole process is repeated until the program itself is terminated. Save the program and run it to see the output in the shell area.

To terminate the program, simply click the red 'Stop' icon. The program will terminate without ever being able to reach the last line of the code.

Using conditionals and variables

Open up a new project by clicking the 'New' icon and in the scripts area, input the following line of code

userName = input ("What is your name? ")

Save the program and run it. The output of this program is that it displays a message asking for your name. After the end of the message, left-click the empty space, write a name, and hit ENTER. Nothing will happen in the program, but if you shift your focus to the right towards the variables window, you'll see that a variable 'userName' assigned with the value you just entered has been created.

To demonstrate how to use variables in python, we will pair the 'userName' variable with a conditional statement. In this demonstration, the program will ask us for our name, and based on our answer, it will give us a specific response.

```
if userName == "Clark Kent":

print("You are Superman!")

else:


print("You are not Superman!")
```

Now run the program after saving it and notice the output. In the first scenario, when the program asks us for our name, it compares it with the variable's value "Calrk Kent" to see if it matches. If our name matches the one in the variable, then the condition is said to be True; if it does not match, then the condition is said to be False. Depending on the result being True or False, the conditional statement instructs the program to execute one of the following lines of code.

Also, notice that instead of one equality "=" symbol, we used a double equality symbol "==." This is because a single equality symbol actually assigns a value to a variable, or in simpler terms, makes this value equal to this variable. While the double equality symbol makes a direct comparison. One is an assigning operator, while the other is a comparative operator.

Also, a text in quotation marks is referred to as a String. A number with or without quotation marks is referred to as an Integer. When you are combining two different types of information, for example, the text "How old are you?" with the reply 22, you will have to convert the integer into a string before they can be joined.

When working with numbers, you can also use the greater than '>' and lesser than '<' comparative operators. But to use the equal to operator, you'll have to use '==.' Similarly, equal to or greater than '=>' and equal to or less than '=<' can also be used.

We will now use some comparison operators in the loop example we used before.

while userName != "Clark Kent":

print("You are not Superman – try again!")

userName = input ("what is your name")

print("You are Superman!)

Upon running this program, you'll see that instead of quitting the program after telling you that you are not superman, it will keep inquiring your name until it is confirmed that you are indeed the superhero Superman.

How to Use Raspberry Pi

How to Interface Our Electronics

Keep in mind that the Raspberry Pi device is going to be able to help us out with measuring out a lot of different things, including the voltage, current, and resistance.

Some of these will include:

1. Diodes:

This is going to be a semiconductor component that simply allows one current to flow in one direction and ensures that this current is not allowed to flow the other direction.

2. Light-emitting diodes or LEDs:

This LED is going to act in a similar manner as a diode, just that it emits light of some color if the current flows in the right direction.

There are many colors, sizes, and shapes for you to choose from with the LEDs.

The length of the leg is going to determine which of the legs is positive and which one is negative.

3. Capacitors:

A capacitor is going to be a component that can be used in order to store some of the electrical energy that you need.

This can be useful when you want to store energy when there is a big difference in voltage between the two plates.

Once the difference in voltage is able to dissipate, it is going to help to release the energy that is stored to ensure that it doesn't harm the Pi device.

4. Transistors:

A transistor is going to be a semiconductor component that can be used to amplify or switch electricity or electric signals.

5. Optocouplers:

These are helpful because they are going to be digital switching devices that ensure that you are able to isolate two electrical circuits from one another.

6. Switches and buttons:

These are going to be pretty self-explanatory.

These are going to be the input devices that you interact with to make sure that the circuit does something.

Understanding Communication Protocols

Some of the most important concepts that we are able to work with when it comes to these communication protocols include:

1. Bitrate:

This is going to be the part that helps us to describe how many bits are sent per unit of time.

2. Band rate:

While we are going to use the bit rate is able to describe the number of bits that we have, the band rate is going to help us to describe how many symbols are going to be sent per unit of time that we want to use.

The symbols can each come in as any number of bits that we want, and it often depends on the design that we work with.

3. Parallel communication:

When we work with this one, the bits are going to be sent out so that just one goes out at the same time.

4. Serial communication:

This is going to be a type of communication where the bits will be sent out just one at a time.

5. Synchronous serial communication:

This is going to be the protocol that we are able to use for serial communication where all of the data that we are going to use will be sent out in a stream that is continuous and steady.

This is going to require that the internal clocks of the systems that we embed will be synchronized at the same rate to help the receiver get all of the signals at regular intervals.

6. Asynchronous serial communication:

When we are working with this one, we will find that this will not require us to have an internal clock that is synchronized.

This data stream is going to contain some of the start and the stop signals that happen before and after the transmission, respectively.

When we get it so that the receiver starts with the right start signal, it is going to then prepare them for the incoming data stream.

But when the signal to stop comes in, it is going to reset itself so that it can be open to a new stream coming in at a later time.

How to Capture Images, Videos, and Images

The first option that we are able to work with is how to use the Raspberry Pi for images and videos.

If you have the right extras to work with it, it is even possible for us to work with videos that are high in quality as well. this stream, when it is done using the device, you will be able to view it in an asynchronously.

The only limit that we are going to see here will be the duration because if you are short on storage, you are not going to be able to tape a very long video.

To get started with this, though, we need to take the time to add a camera to your device.

You can go through and either use a USB webcam, or you can go through and purchase a camera that has been built in order to work specifically with your Pi device.

We are going to work with the option for the Raspberry Pi Camera to help make this quick and not waste time with the explanation here, but you will find that the work that comes with adding on some of the other options of cameras will be similar.

To help us get started with this process, we need to make sure that we are able to get the camera of our choice attached to the Pi device.

There are going to be a few different options that we are able to use with this one including:

1. Turn the device off.

Make sure that you don't touch the metal contacts of your ribbon cable, or you might ruin it.

2. Take the lens protector off.

3. Get the CSI connector and then gently pull up the housing clip.

This is going to be either white or black.

4. Insert the CSI cable into its slot.

5. Now you can push down the housing clip in order to let it get locked in place.

6. Now that this is in place, you can turn the Pi device pack on and configure the camera.

You will be able to enable the camera with the following command:

pi@erpi ~ $ sudo raspi-config

7. Reboot the device.

If you would like to go through and capture images, you would need to input the following command:

pi@erpi ~ $ raspistill -o image.jpg

pi@erpi ~ $ ls -l image.jpg

Of course, this is just the start of what we are going to do when it is time to set up this system and make sure that it is running in the right manner as well.

It is also possible for us to go through and set up our own security system for the home or even stream some videos with this feature as well if we would like.

There are a lot of great things that we are able to do with the camera and the webcam being on the Pi device, but there are a few more steps that we will need to discuss later on in order to get all of this set up to work.

How to Record and Play Audio

For the most part, when you are doing the necessary work to take the videos that you would like, you have to make sure that there is some noise or audio that comes with it to make them actually work.

And then there are times when maybe you would like to just add in the audio that you want to use.

Sometimes, you will want to add in a speaker, for example, to help the Pi device to play music or use other noises along the way.

And we are going to now look at the steps that we can take in order to make sure we can do this audio work.

So, to make sure that we are able to get the audio set up and ready to go, we have to make sure that we are getting the audio input or output device ready to go.

The cool thing to work with here is that the Pi device is going to come with its own built-in audio output system in most of the versions, and then these are going to connect right to the device with the help of the port of the HDMI.

For input, though, we need to work with an additional device to make this happen.

Some of the options that we are able to use to make this happens to include:

1. The USB audio:

For this project to work, we need to be able to attach an input device with USB audio.

This can be done as long as you pick out one that is able to work with some of the drivers of Linux.

You may also work with some of the webcams of USB that we talked about before.

We just have to go with one that comes with a microphone to make it work.

2. Bluetooth Audio:

The next thing that we are able to use here is either the audio input that works directly with Bluetooth, or you need to go with an output system in order to help connect back to the Pi device.

We just need to make sure, like with the above, that we are choosing one that will be compatible with the Linux system for the best results.

3. Raspberry Pi HATs:

These are going to be known as the shorthand for Hardware Attached on Top.

You are able to choose to attach one of these in order to use the various capabilities of audio that are going to be available with the Pi device.

If you would like to go through and ensure that the recording you do will have audio and work well, then you have to go through and ensure the ALSA utility software is found on your device.

This is a good software to have because it will have the play and the record utilities that are necessary for us to get all of the audio that we need.

To help us out if we still need to install this software on our own device, we can use the coding below:

pi@erpi ~ $ sudo apt update

pi@erpi ~ $ sudo apt install alsa-utils

And this should be enough to get it downloaded.

You may need to go through and reboot the Pi device to make sure that it gets on the program the way that you would like.

Now, we need to take a quick look at how you can use this software, and the tools that come with it, in order to record and to play the audio that you need with either your own movies or with your music.

To record the audio, you just need to use the following command:

pi@erpi ~/tmp $ arecord -f ed -D plughw:1,0 -d 10 test.wav

And then, when you are ready to make sure that the audio is going to play, you just need to work with the following command:

pi@erpi ~ /tmp # aplay -D plughw:1,0 test.wav

As we are able to see here, there are a ton of options that we are able to focus on when we bring in the Raspberry Pi device, and we are ready to make it work for our needs.

There are so many projects and more that we are able to do with this controller, and as long as we are set up and ready to go with it, we are likely to get the results that we want in no time.

Projects made with Raspberry Pi (Part 1)

The Arcade Box

Some of the different supplies and options that we need to keep around when creating our own arcade box will include:

- A game controller is not necessary, but it can make playing some of the games a little bit easier.

- A power supply so that the device turns on

- The Raspberry Pi 3 (or other Raspberry Pi device that you want to use)

- A good SD card (This card needs to be at least 4GB in order to make the games work.)

- An HDMI cable to hook your device up to a monitor

- A TV

Step 1

Get the games from the RetroPie website over to your PI.

We are going with the RetroPie website to help us get some of the older games that we are going to use for this device.

- You will simply need to download the website over to your SD card so that it can then be put on the Pi device.

- To do this, visit retropie.org.uk/download, and from there, you can pick out the version of the Raspberry device that you want to work with.

- Give it some time to copy over to your SD card.

Step 2.

Once everything is over on the SD card, you can turn on the Raspberry device.

Step 3.

Add in the controller and plug the device into the television while you wait for it to load up.

Step 4.

Add the SD card inside the device and give it a few minutes to boot up.

If you did the conversion properly, then you should see the EmulationStation come up on the television screen.

As we start to work on this step, and we get something to show up on the screen, we can then go through and make sure that any and all the configurations that are necessary here are going to be complete.

The controller is often going to be the best way to handle this because it can make things easier.

And when we work on the controller, it is possible just to go through and click on only the things that we need before finishing it all up.

The first time that we do this is going to take a bit of time because we have never done it before, but the more times we must go through it, the faster the project will go.

After we have been able to go through and get the Wi-Fi hooked up and ready to go to our device, and you are certain that you have gotten it started up and ready to go, then it is time to add on the ROMS part to this device as well.

Getting this setup and running is going to take a few moments, but the process is simple and pretty like what we did before.

To do this, we either need to make sure that we have a nice strong internet connection, or we can use an Ethernet cord.

If your connection is not strong, and the ROMS does get interrupted at all, then you will end up with some messy problems to try and fix.

It is your choice, but often it is best to at least do this part with the Ethernet cord to prevent issues.

Step 5.

Go onto your main computer.

If you are using a Windows computer, you can open up into the file manager on the computer and type in a simple code of "//retropie".

If you are working with a Mac computer, you can go to the finder on the computer, select on Go, and then click on Connect to Server.

Step 6.

You would then type in the code "smb://retropie".

Both of these end up with the same results—they just have to be done a bit differently on different computers.

At this point, we should have the Wi-Fi and other parts connected properly, and that is when we are going to be able to handle the ROMS over on our device.

We should do this in a remote manner, so that means that we can use the SD card to move our chosen games over, or we are able to choose which games we are going to use the most often and have those get put directly on the Raspberry Pi device.

Turning the Device into a Phone

The second project that we can spend some time on is turning our Raspberry Pi device into a phone.

This is easier to do than it may seem, though we have to keep in mind that it is not going to be the most advanced phone.

We will not be creating a phone like a smartphone or anything like that, but it will be able to send and receive calls and even do some basic texting, which can be cool.

To get started with this one, we need to make sure that we have the right tools, and those include:

- Headphones

- Microphone

- An electrical switch

- Velcro squares to help hook it all together

- A touch screen

- GSM module that has an antenna and some audio outlets

- Battery pack to help power the phone

- A Raspberry Pi 3 that can handle the Python coding language

- Duct tape

- Cables

- Zip ties

- A sim card

- A converter for DC-DC

- A foam board that you are able to cut down to be the same size as the Raspberry Pi

When you are picking out the supplies that you need for this project, you should double-check that they are going to be compatible with the Pi 3 and not one of the other versions of Raspberry Pi.

There are a lot of choices out there in terms of the supplies that you can use, and many of them come in at a lower price.

But you want to make sure that they are of high enough quality, and that they are actually going to work with the device that you want to use.

After we make sure that we have all of the right supplies that will work with our Raspberry Pi device, it is time to make sure that the software we need it put on the device as well.

For this to work, we need to bring in that Python that we talked about earlier, so make sure that this language has been added to our Raspberry Pi device as well.

While we are on this process, we need to make sure that we add on a few other types of software as well, including PiPhone and the WireHunt, so that it will be easier to turn this simple board into the phone that we want to use.

The easiest way for us to add these pieces of software to our device is to add them to the SD card we want to use first and then just transferring those over at that time.

Now that all of these items are present and ready to go, it is time for us to start turning the device into a phone that we are able to use.

Step 1.

Connect our battery so that the board, or our phone, will be able to start up.

We need to do this over a switch so that the batter is going to end up with the necessary power.

Step 2.

Once we have this done, it is time to hook both of these to the GSM module.

Take the header of the GSM and then connect it over to the converter that you are using as well.

Step 3.

Once we have been able to go through and connect all of these together, it is now time to hook them up to the Raspberry Pi device that we want to work with we are able to use this with some of the other cables that you should have.

The first part of all of this is to connect the device with the other transmit pins to ensure that they are going to stay with one another.

Check that the pins are all connected to the T and the Rx ports.

While this is going to require us to connect quite a few parts together, once we get this done, and can work with the SIM card, then we are good to go.

Step 4.

Now that all of our lines have had time to be connected and our SIMs card is actually in place, it is now time for us to go through and actually assemble all of the parts.

To make sure that this is going to work, we need to bring out that piece of foam that is on our list, and then slice it to be the same size as our Pi device.

Step 5.

Place the device over this piece of foam and then use the squares of Velcro and some duct tape to get the two parts to be together.

This step is important because it is going to help us to connect the converter, the switch, and the module to the other side of our piece of foam you have to make sure that when you add on the battery pack that it goes to a place that is secure usually somewhere between the Pi device and the screen.

You do not want to have it so that the battery pack is going to move around and cause some trouble.

If it moves around, then the phone will turn off randomly and cause issues along the way.

At this point, if you actually went through and connected all of the parts in the proper manner, then you should notice that our phone is going to be done for the most part here, and you should be able to turn it on and get it to actually work.

Turning on the Phone

To turn on the phone, you can just turn on the switch that goes to the phone, and it should turn on.

From here, you can wait for it to turn on and boot up before dialing any number that you want and use this to make a simple phone call to someone else.

As we can imagine here, this is going to be a pretty simple kind of phone to work with.

We just set it up to do some simple processes, and it is not going to be all that complicated or have any of the features that we want or are used to with some of the other phones that we may have used in the past.

But we are able to use this basic phone to help us make and then receive the codes that we would like, just like a regular phone.

The neat thing is that we can take this a bit further if we would like.

For this project, we are just keeping it simple with a phone that can make and receive the calls that we want.

But it is possible to take this simple phone and set it up to do some other options, like texting and even getting online and so much more.

This just goes to prove that the Raspberry Pi is able to take on a lot of diverse processes if you would like, and it can even, with a few simple steps, go enough that it helps us to make our own phones.

It is simple to use, and with just a few, and inexpensive accessories, we are able to do so much.

We can use it to create an arcade game to play some of our old favorite games anywhere we go, and even to help us make calls with our own phone that we can make.

And there are so many other projects that we are able to do with the same idea, and a few different attachments, along the way.

Projects made with Raspberry Pi (Part 2)

The Quiz Game

The program shown below that exemplifies the keyboard event is a game of questions and answers, also using various sources of funds. See the code:

Set 2 - Pygame Quiz

1 import pygame, sys

2 from pygame.locals import *

3 pygame.init () pygame module #starts

4 = blue (0.0255) #color blue

5 blank = (255,255,255) #White color

6 pygame.display.set_mode screen = ((800,600)) #define window size

7 pygame.font.Font source = ("Freesansbold.ttf" 15) #define source to be used

8 instruction = "Pygame Quiz: Press the letter of the correct answer" #instruction

9 subquestion1 = "What is the capital of USA? a) Washington DC) b) Newyork c) San Jose d) and New jersey)" #first question

10 subquestion2 = "What is the capital of France? a) London b) Paris c) Tokyo d) and Madrid) Lisbon" #second question

11 subquestion3 = "What is the capital of China? a) Shanghai) b) New York c) Berlin) d) and Beijing)" #third question

12 result = "" #inform informing result (empty starts)

13 questions = [Subquestion1, subquestion2, subquestion3] #list containing questions

14 = answers [Pygame.K_a, pygame.K_b, pygame.K_d] #list containing the keys of the answers to the questions

15 question_number = 0 # Variable that controls which question appears

16 continue = true # Variable that controls the flow repeat

17 result_view = false # Controlling the second variable flow repeat

```
18 while continue == true: # Repeat loop

19 screen.fill (White) #paint the screen with white color

20 start_text = source.render (instruction, True, blue)
        #define statement text
21 screen.blit (start_text, (50,50)) #show text with the
        onscreen instructions
22    text    =    source.render    (questions
        [number_question] True, blue) #define which
        question list is displayed and the text form

23 screen.blit (text, (0.100)) #show the question on the screen

24 is in pygame.event.get () event: #capture all events

25 if event.type == QUIT: #check if the exit event

26 continue = false # No longer perform the first repeat loop

27 result_view = false # No longer perform the second loop
```

```
28 if event.type == pygame.KEYDOWN: #check if the
event key press

29 if event.key == [question_number] answers:
        #Checks if pressed key is the question answer
30 if question_number <2: #If is not the last question
list

31 = 1 + question_number #pass to the next question

32 else: #If is the last question list

33 continue = false # Stops executing the first loop

34 display_result = true #enable second loop

35 result = "Congratulations you won!" #message
result

36 else: #If the pressed key is not the correct answer

37 continue = false #to performing first loop

38 display_result = true #enable second loop

39 result = "Answer wrong, you lost!" #message result
```

40 pygame.display.update () #updates display

41 while result_view == true: #Second repeat loop

42 is in pygame.event.get () event: #capture all events

43 if event.type == QUIT: #check if the exit event

44 result_view = false # No longer perform the loop

45 text = font.render (result, True, blue) #mounts text with the result

46 screen.blit (text, (100,200)) #views text on the screen

47 pygame.display.update () #updates display

48 pygame.quit () #ends the program

In this game are presented questions of countries and capitals. There are three questions in sequence; if you miss some, you lose; if you hit all wins. They have three options, letters a, b, c: the player must press one of these on the keyboard.

Game Components

In lines 8-11, the texts are set to be used: the instruction to the player and the three questions with your possible answers. Variables: subquestion1, subquestion2, and subquestion3 form a list (or array) later. The outcome variable (line 12) will be used to display text indicating whether you won or lost; at first, she gets "empty."

As the games run on repetition ties, work with lists is advantageous. Thus, according to the action, you only need to change the list index instead of changing variables. For questions is inserted into a list called questions (line 13), which will bring together the variables of the three questions, similarly, a list of the answers to the name of the key inserted in the correct answers (line 14). The first question answer is the first element of the list answers, and so on. A list needs an index, for it is created query_number variable; the first position of a list to zero, so query_number is initialized to 0 (line 15).

By repeating the main loop (line 18), the text is mounted on the instructions initial_text variable (line 20) using the source (which is defined in line 7) blue. On line 21, this text will be drawn on the screen at (50.50). It is made the same for the first question is assembled with the variable text question to be made and used the same source and the same color (lines 22 and 23). The question, removed from the variable list question, is the first because the index (the variable_question number) is worth 0.

Line 28 checks the occurrence of the event press of a key (KeyDown), if there is a line 29 compares the key (event.key) pressed with the list of answers; if the same index pointed to by question_number, you must also check if it is the last question (line 30). As the third question index is 2, question_number is less than 2 (not the last question), then the program adds 1 to the variable question_number (line 31); with this, the next iteration will come the following question from the list.

If the index is equal to question_number 2 (in else), is the last question and already can display the result of the match (line 32): the variable continues receiving false (line 33) to exit the main loop; the variable display_result receive true (line 34) to enter the second loop, and the variable result gets "Congratulations! You won" (line 35). If the key pressed (event.key) does not match the correct answer (line 36), the variable continues to receive false (line 37) out of the main loop; the variable display_result receives true to enter the second loop (line 38), and the variable result gets "Answer wrong, you lost" (line 39).

In lines 41 to 47 is the second repeat loop, which shows the result of the game to close the program. It performs as the variable display_result is true. The phrase of the variable result (indicating whether won or lost) is rendered in blue and assigned to the variable text (line 45), which is mounted in position (100,200) of the screen (line 46).

Time Function And Animation

So far, the program repeat loop indefinitely performed several times a second. But we exercised no control over it. This means that the speed of an object can vary from computer to computer, according to the hardware that runs the program.

The pygame lets you control the amount of time the program runs per second. You need to set a variable to control the time (e.g., variable_of_time), and they must get the pygame.time.Clock () command. The method tick () of this variable defines the number of times that the program must perform per second, for example, variable_of_time.tick (30).

This program moves a ball from one corner to the other, moving one pixel at a time, doing it thirty times per second.

This ball is loaded, and two variables are created for the ball position 0 for both receiving the ball starts in the upper left corner of the screen (lanes 7 to 9). The ball must have a size 50 by 50 pixels.

In line 10, insert a variable called to move the ball movement_horizontal, which can have the value 1 or - 1. When added to the horizontal_position variable, it will move the ball to the left or right. Soon after, you insert a variable time clock call (line 11).

If the value of the horizontal_position variable reaches 750 (which is the screen width less than the width of the ball), the horizontal_position variable gets -1 for the ball back to the left (lines 16 and 17). But if the position the ball gets to zero, the horizontal_ movement variable gets 1 for the ball to go right (lines 18 and 19). Thus the ball will be going back and forth on the screen without leaving it.

In line 20, the horizontal_position variable (started with 0) may increase or decrease according to the horizontal_position value; this variable horizontal_position starts with a value of 1 to horizontal_position starting increasing, taking the ball to the right. When horizontal_position reaches 750, the horizontal_position variable becomes negative, causing the ball back to the left.

In line 24, the use of a long variable named clock 30 and passed to its method tick (); you will repeat the main loop to run 30 times a second. If this value is increased, you can see that the ball increases your speed on the screen.

Animations

To date, we move objects on the screen. The objects, however, were not animated, did not own movements. The animations are very common in games, and we can do it also with pygame. Like in the movies, the animations are the display of several consecutive images in a short time. The human eye can see 30 frames per second; some games, however, use 60 or more frames per second.

For the next program, we will require consecutive images.

These images show the movement of a character running. With an image editor, you can separate this image in 4 others (see the next Figure), each containing a time of character movement. Record them with the names athlete1, athlete2, athlete3, athlete4.

Projects Made with Raspberry Pi (Part 3)

Home Arcade Box

Who doesn't want an arcade box at home? Even though the Raspberry Pi isn't powerful enough to support modern games it still has the ability to run the classics. Emulators are available online which can help you support outdated consoles like the Sega Genesis, SNES or even the PlayStation PC which is available on CD ROMs. Though most of us run Raspberry Pi on Raspbian Operating Systems, guys from RetroPie spent a lot of time in developing and recreating custom disk image to play some of the older titles. Road Rash anyone?

This is a pretty simple tutorial on how to achieve maximum gaming. What you will need:

- Raspberry Pi

- USB controller

- Micro SD Card- At least 4 GB

- TV

- HDMI or AV Cables

- Power Supply

NOTE: You can find a list of all compatible accessories on the Raspberry Pi Wiki.

The first step is to download and install RetroPi on your SD card.

You will do this by visiting https://retropie.org.uk/download/ and clicking on the version of Raspberry Pi that you have. When it is done downloading you need to extract the image to your SD card. If you are using Windows, try Win32DiskImager and for Mac try RPI-SD Card Builder. Then remove the SD card and place it into your Pi.

After this you will need to boot up your Raspberry Pi. Plug your keyboard and controller in your Pi, insert the SD card and boot it up. After a few minutes, it should boot directly to the EmulationStation and this is where you configure your controller. Since it is the first time you are turning it on, you will need to follow the prompts to set up the controller. When that is done, you can use your controller to pilot through your emulators and RetroPie. Here you can also set hot keys for frequently used actions such as save and exit.

Next you will set up your Wi-Fi, scroll down to "Configure Wi-Fi" and use the action button to select it. Click on "Set Up Network", select your network, type in your passcode, and hit okay.

Next you will copy your ROMs over to your Pi. To do this you should make sure your internet connection is working properly. Then, if you are using Windows, open file manager and type in //retropie and if you are using a Mac open your finder, select Go> Connect to Server, type in smb://retropie, and connect. Now you will be able to easily remotely transfer ROM's from one device to the another! Once everything is transferred, reboot you Pi with your controller plugged in and you should be good to go!

- TIP: If you would much rather use a USB drive to store your ROM's it is very simple to do. Put them on the USB drive in a folder called "retropie" and then plug it in!

Make your own phone

With a similar phones popping in every corner, we are lacking of choice between iPhone, android and a Windows phone. Then it time to make you own PiPhone! Thanks to Raspberry Pi's versatility, it is able to make host of connections and turning it into your new phone is not going to take too much effort. All you need to buy is a battery pack, as GSM module, a compatible touch screen and you have all the hardware requirements to create your next new phone. You can run your phone on the software already available in the market or hook up with some tutorials online to connect to all Apple store, Google play and the Microsoft Apps. Or simply download the apk file and run it with your smartphone. Although, this is not considered a difficult project, it does require many different items and some of them can be expensive, just keep that in mind when you begin. Here is what you will need:

- Duct tape

- Cables

- Zip ties

- Sim card

- 5 VC DC-DC converter

- Foam board, cut to the size of the Raspberry Pi

- Headphones

- Microphone

- Electrical switch

- Velcro squares

- Touch screen

- GSM/GPRS module with antenna and audio outlets

- Battery Pack

- Raspberry Pi running Python

First, you will need to put everything on the Raspberry Pi, as mentioned above, Python will be used as well as Piphone software which is available for free online and Wirehunt, also a free download. So, the first step is to put all of this on the Raspberry Pi. Once, all of this is on the device, connect it to the touchscreen.

Now you will need power, so use the cables and connect the battery to the switch, then connect the switch to the GSM module. Next, you will need to connect the GSM header to the DC-DC converter. Now, you will need to link this to the Raspberry Pi using another cable. The Raspberry Pi will also need to be connected via cables from the transmit pins to the GSM module as well, these are also known as the Rx and Tx ports. Once this has been completed, simply insert the sim card.

Now you will need to assemble the parts, begin by placing the Raspberry Pi on the foam board. Use the Velcro squares and the duct tape to attach the GSM module, converter, and the switch on the other side of the foam. Put the battery between the screen and the Raspberry Pi, but make sure not to leave it turned on for all of this because it can get too hot.

Now, everything is ready to be used. Just turn it on and dial a number you wish to call. Remember, this is just a basic phone. What you choose to do with it from here is up to you, but this gave you a great starting foundation. Some people choose to use software that allows them to run Android or Apple apps. There are many different possibilities.

More Projects with Raspberry Pi (Part 4)

Raspberry Pi XBMC

XBMC is the most popular of all media streaming centers and it is dead easy to get it onto your Raspberry Pi 3. You will need some extra materials:

- Raspberry Pi 3

- 3.5mm stereo audio cable – optional – only needed if your video output is analog and you require external speakers or are going to use the speakers on your TV. If you opt of r HDMI, you won't need this cable

- Card reader (external or use the one built-in to your computer if present)

- Ethernet cable

- HDMI video cable (or composite, your choice)

- Micro USB power supply – 5V 2A is best

- Minimum 8 GB Class 10 microSD card

- Raspberry Pi case – this is optional but it will protect your Pi 3

- Raspbmc Installer – for getting the right version of XBMC for Raspberry Pi 3 onto your card. You could use OSMC if you prefer.

- Remote control, only if you don't intend using your mouse and keyboard for controlling your media center

- USB Hard drive – an optional extra, for use in storing video if you prefer not to stream from another PC

- USB mouse and keyboard

XBMC is incredibly powerful as a media center and the Pi 3 is the best choice for running it on but, you need to be aware that there are a few things that it cannot do. For a start, it cannot stream any content that comes via the internet and you won't get perfect video at 1080p. that said 720p is fine and much of what you get is going to depend on where the audio is played from – it is better to stream from a USB drive than it is the network.

Some of the menus will likely be slower and don't expect brilliant skins because you won't get them. However, it is perfectly adequate as a backup media center so let's get own with building it.

Step 1 - Install Raspbmc

This is the very first step and we are going to put it on your microSD card. This is how it's done in Windows:

- Put the microSD into your card reader

- Download the installer and save it to your desktop.

- Run it by double-clicking the icon

- Download the files to your card and then use the safe eject feature on your computer to remove the card.

Step 2 – Hook up your Raspberry Pi 3 and install Raspbmc

Next, we need to connect the Pi 3 to the television so plug in the HDMI cable to the Pi 3 and connect it to the TV. Insert the Ethernet cable and connect it to your router and then insert the SD card and connect the power cable to a power source. Turn on Raspberry Pi 3 and it will boot from your SD card. Raspbmc will now install to your Pi 3.

Don't touch anything while the installation is taking place – it will take about 1 to 25 minutes so leave it to finish, at which point it will boot up to XBMC.

Step 3 – Tweak Your Settings

Nearly there, we just need to change a few settings so that it all runs right. These are the recommended settings:

- Resolution - open Settings>System>Video Output. Change to the resolution you want – 720p is best.

- Overscan – open Settings>System>Video Output>Video Calibration. Use the calibration wizard to get the picture fitting the screen

- System Performance Profile – open Programs>Raspbmc Settings>System Configuration. This is a setting that is specific to the Pi 3, allowing you to overclock so things are a little bit faster. Set it to "Fast" as this will make things speedier but won't affect the stability. "Super" setting runs things even faster but is liable to cause some instability

- MPEG2 Codec License – This must be bought via the Raspberry Pi store. Once purchased, open Programs>Raspbmc Settings>System Configuration to set it up. You can play videos in MPEG 2 – these cannot be played on the Pi as it is. If you are not using these videos, you can ignore this step.

Your XBMC center is now set and ready to go.

Minecraft Server

While running Minecraft on the Raspberry Pi might not be the most satisfying experience, you can run a Minecraft server on it. You and a few of your friends can play using the RPi 4 as a server, but you do need to keep in mind that this is a small computer. Try to avoid things like entities on the ground, an absurd amount of pets, and complex red stone contraptions.

If you run into a problem running it on the RPi 4, then make sure you consult this page as it has helped others with a recurring issue regarding Java

eBook Library

Do you love books, including eBooks? Do your friends love eBooks? Then you might want a portable eBook library where you can share eBooks with others on the go.

RetroPie

This is my favorite project. It is not difficult to set up, and the increased processing power and graphics of the Raspberry Pi 4 make it even better than on the Raspberry Pi 3 B+. The RetroPie software allows you to play "retro" games, e.g. Atari, C64, NES, Sega Genesis, and more!

The most difficult part about set up is downloading an image to an SD card. Once it is up and running you can use retro controllers as well, which really makes the experience nostalgic.

Tip: The RPi 4 can get hot running non-intensive programs, and RetroPie is something can make it work a little. Make sure you have a fan for your RPi 4. The last thing you want to do is at best throttle its performance and at worst damage the life span of your RPi 4.

Overclocking

Overclocking is one of the most common projects people do with their Raspberry Pi. Overclocking is just the process of boosting your CPU. This isn't without its drawbacks. You'll need to make sure you have an above par power supply, and you'll need a fan (something you already need with the RPi 4.

Heat Sink and Fan

This project is actually a necessity for the RPi 4 because of the heat issues. There are tons of options for this from how many heat sinks you put on to what type of fan you use for cooling. Heat sinks are super simple to attach, and fans are only marginally more difficult.

You can use small heat sinks, large heat sinks, small fans, fans in cases, external fans, etc. It really is up to you on which you pick, but make sure you do pick a heat   sink   and   fan.

More Projects with Raspberry Pi (Part 5)

Game Emulator

Before you can begin, you are going to need to gather your equipment. Here is a list of the things that you are going to need to have in order to create your game emulator.

- A game controller with USB connectors
- A Raspberry Pi 3 Model B board
- The proper cables that will allow you to hook your board into the HDMI ports on the TV or monitor that you are going to be playing on.
- A case for your Raspberry board
- Keyboard and mouse that offers you a USB connection
- Micro SD card
- The HDMI cable that you are going to hook into your display device

- A power supply for the board

1. The primary thing that you are going to do is download the retro Pie project onto the hard drive of your computer. You will be able to obtain the download file on the retro Pie website.

2. At this point, you will need to download another image by the name of Win32DiskImager. After this has been downloaded, you will take the retro Pie file that is on your hard drive and move it to the SD card that you gathered when you were getting all your equipment together. Before you write the image onto the SD card, you should ensure that you have the details correct so that you are not writing the image somewhere that it does not need to be.

3. Once you have the image printed onto the SD card, you will remove that SD card from your computer and put it into your Pi board. From here, you are also going to

connect everything to the appropriate ports so that you do not have to do it later.

4. Your PI should automatically boot up the retro Pie. After it has booted up, you are going to need to press F4 so that you get the command prompt opened on your screen.

5. After the command prompt has opened, you will enter the code: sudo rasPi config

6. The expanded file system needs to be selected before you hit accept.

7. Now back to your main screen, you will go to options and locate the SSH option under the advanced options. If it is not already authorized, you will need to enable it.

8. Moving on to overclock, you will choose medium unless you are playing games that have graphics that are more complex, in this case, you are going to Pick the higher option.

9. Just like always, you will finish with your options and then reboot your board.

10. After the restart is done, you are going to go to the main screen which is now going to be able to load your game emulators.

11. Your Pi board needs to be connected to your home network, and after you have ensured that it is connected, you will need to go to your network that is in the windows explorer. There should be a table of devices that are attached to the network, and you will need to go to the one that is labeled RaspberryPi. You will need to double click it.

12. There is going to be a folder titled ROMS, and this is going to be the folder where all your games are going to be stored as they pertain to the game emulator.

13. Your ROMS must be unzipped before you are able to load them where they need to be loaded.

Please remember that if you do not have access to your Raspberry Pi because of the connection that it has to your internet, you can try one of these solutions.

- Take an empty USB drive and plug it into your Raspberry Pi 3 board.

- Wait until the light quits flashing before you pull the USB out of the port on your board and plug it into your machine.

- There should be an empty directory on the USB that is constructed just for the ROM files that you want to play.

- The ROM files that you have unzipped will need to be coPied and placed into their appropriate directories on your USB drive.

- Unplug the USB from your computer and plug it back into your Raspberry Pi.

- Once again, wait for the activity light to stop blinking so that you know all the files have been reproduced over on your Raspberry Pi.

Raspberry Pi: Personal Assistant

In order to complete this project, you will need:

- A mouse and keyboard that will attach to your Raspberry Pi 3 board via a USB connector.
- An HDMI cable and a television that supports HDMI.
- A Raspberry Pi 3 board that already has Raspbian Wheezy installed on it.
- Extra wires.
- A Wi-Fi adapter with a USB connection.
- A double pole double is thrown relays that run off five volts.
- A USB soundcard
- Part of a vero board
- A five-volt power supply
- A five-volt amplifier, you are going to want to keep this small so that it can be held close to your Pi board.
1. Update your Raspberry Pi board; you will need to connect your board to your network via an ethernet cable so that you

are getting faster speeds than if you were just working off a Wi-Fi connection.

2. After you have updated your board, you will need to shut it down so that the new updates are applied.

3. Before using the power back on to your board, you are going to need to connect your Wi-Fi adaptor.

4. Once booted up, go to the desktop and select the option that is going to allow you to configure your Wi-Fi settings. From here a new window is going to be opened.

5. Select the scan button so that another new window is opened.

6. In this window, you will go to the SSID and double click it.

7. A third window is going to be opened, and you are going to need to enter your password into the PSK box before clicking add.

8. Moving back to the first window that opened, you will be able to check the IP

address and see that you are connected to your wireless network.

9. Shut your Pi board down once more.

After you have done that, you will be ready to set up the hardware that is associated with creating your personal assistant.

1. Open the plastic case for your sound card; you are going to desolder some of the connectors. You will need to solder where the connectors are so you are not harming the actual sound card components.

2. Taking your DPDT relais, you are going to make the push button on the intercom that you have gotten and connect the DPDT to that button. The second wire that is attached to the switch will need to go into the relay coil while the first wire goes to the ground. This way whenever the button is pushed, you are activating the coil and relay switches. You can also add a diode in the opposite direction over your two Pins that are connected to the coil.

3. The Pins that are in the middle of your DPDT relays are going to have a positive and negative connection that is going to go to your speaker. The Pins that are usually open are going to be attached to the microphone's input for the soundcard. The Pins that are normally closed will be the output of the soundcard. However, you may find that the signal for your output is not going to be loud enough, therefore you need to have your amplifier.

4. Take the five-volt Pin for your amplifier and the five-volt GND Pin and connect them so that you now have power flowing through your amplifier from the soundcard. You will need to connect the R+ to the R- to the Pins that are typically closed in your relay.

5. After you have done this, put everything into the intercom case and then connect your sound card to your Raspberry Pi board.

6. It is not recommended that you try to power everything from your board, that is why you may want to consider getting a three amp wall adapter. Depending on the wall adaptor that you get will depend on if you must cut the connector to the adaptor and connect a USB connector so that you can power your board.

7. After you have cooked everything up, you will need to close the case for your intercom.

8. Take your sound card and configure it by opening your configuration file. You can do this by putting this code into your command prompt. Sudo nano/ etc/ mod probe. d/alsa- base . conf.

9. The part of your code that says: options snd- USB- audio index = -2 to where it says the same thing except your index is going to be 0.

10. Reboot your Pi board so that the new changes can be applied.

You are now at the point that you are going to be setting up the software that you need to run your voice commands.

1. It is recommended that you use the Steven Hickson voice command software that is going to allow you to have an easy setup and simple to use interface all while being reliable for whatever it is that you are using it for. The software can be located on his website and downloaded for you to use.

2. After you have installed the appropriate voice software, you will input this command. Voice command -s

3. It is with this command that you are going to be able to use the setup wizard and go through it to set up the voice command that is appropriate for your device.

4. After set up you need to enter the voice command -e so that your configure file will open and enable you to set up the commando's that you need and the actions that are related to it.

5. For configuration you will need to enter the script command = = action it is with this command that you are going to be able to set up the commands that you want your personal assistant to do. So, if you say play, then the program is going to know that you want it to play music.

6. After you have completed the editing process for your configuration file, you need to save it. Upon saving, everything is going to be ready for you to use.

7. In order to run the voice command software, you will enter the code voice command-c.

Your personal assistant is now ready to be used! Your personal assistant is going to be able to list to the commands that you give it and execute them appropriately. In the case that your command cannot be executed, then your personal assistant is going to take to the internet and find the answer that you are looking for. Even though your personal assistant can now execute your voice commands, you are not quite done.

1. You are going to make it to where your voice command starts whenever you launch the program. In order to do this, you are going to go to your Raspberry Pi home directory and select the configuration directory.

2. Once in this directory, you are going to create a new list.

3. After it is created, you will need to access this directory.

4. A new file must be created in the directory with this script. Sudo nano voice command. Desktop

5. Open the file you created and insert the code that is going to cause your voice command to start up whenever you execute the program.

[entry for desktop]
Type = application
Name = voicecommand
Exec = voice command – c
Startupnotify = false

6. Ensure your file has been saved before you reboot your Raspberry Pi 3, board.

Raspberry Pi and its History

Raspberry Pi (pronounced raspberry pie) is a tiny computer that has the size of a credit card. Seriously, the Raspberry Pi foundation used an actual credit card to be their template for the design of the printed circuit board (PCB) of this small computer.

Raspberry Pi, or the Pi, or RasPi, or RPi, or whatever nickname you like the most, believe it or not is an actual computer. Its board features the typical hardware that is found in the desktop computers (such as RAM, processor, etc.), which means that this credit card-sized computer also enables you to edit documents, play audio and video, play games, do some coding, etc.

Of course, its tiny size is not able to provide as much power as a normal desktop PC, however, its cheap price of approximately $35 makes up for everything. Actually, the main idea behind the birth of such a computer was to teach kids and adults about the basics of computer science with a minimal investment. It's a lot more convenient to break a Raspberry Pi and replace it with a new one, than learn about the software science with an actual desktop computer and then spend a fortune to replace or fix what you've broken.

Raspberry Pi is as yummy as its sounds. With this tiny computer you can actually move past the 'visible', surface-level software and dive deeply into its 'black box' – the internals that most people are unaware of. Starting the software education with a Raspberry Pi has proven to be the easiest way for people to adopt highly appreciated and super valuable software and hardware engineering skills.

But Raspberry Pi isn't only for these 'academics'. What's even more amazing about this credit card-like computer is that its fan base is super versatile. There are many DIYers and hackers that make Raspberry Pi an essential part of their computer experiments.

A Quick Ride Through History

For those that are simply casually observing the development of the computer technology, it may seem that Raspberry Pi is brand new. And it'd seem like it, since most blogs and websites treat this computer that way. However, the truth is that Raspberry Pi has been around for years. In fact, the creators of the Pi — Rob Mullins, Eben Upton, Alan Mycroft, and Jack Lang — first came with the idea of making a tiny computer in 2006. This came as a result of their observance that the available cheap computers at that time (such as the Amiga or the Spectrum) had a rather negative effect on the programming education, as they were slowing down the ability to learn the software science significantly. And since laptops and desktop computers cost hundreds, some even thousands of dollars, kids back then really couldn't afford to mess with the main family computer that way. So it is only understandable just how much a cheap learning platform was needed.

Trying to realize their idea, the Pi creators played around with various microcontrollers, PCBs, and breadboards, but it wasn't until 2008 that their concept became a reality thanks to the newer technology and cheaper chips. The new powerful tools helped them create a platform that was not only able to teach command-line programming but also supported media. Joined by David Braben and Pete Lomas, the original creators formed the now-popular Raspberry Pi Foundation, and only three years later, in 2011, the first Raspberry Pi hit the market.

With the rise of technology many different models of Raspberry Pi have been created, each of them offering better features than its ancestors.

The Hardware

If you have already purchased your Raspberry Pi, you may have already noticed how 'naked' the device actually comes. Its price may be cheap, about $35, but there are some hidden costs involved. The Pi may be a computer on its own for sure, however, you need a couple of other things to make it work as it should.

A 5V Power Supply. For a device that is USB-powered, everyone can agree that the Raspberry Pi, no matter which flavor you have, is pretty hungry for power. It draws around 600 to 700 mA. And while it can be powered from the USB port – which is rated at around 500 mA, it is important that you use an actual powered adapter. You can use a modern smartphone charger since most of them supply 700 mA at 5V, however, check to see if yours do at the bottom of the charger.

If you don't have a good quality charger, once other devices such as a camera module or a simple Wi-FI dongle are connected, they will draw even more power from the Pi and it may become unstable.

On the other hand, if the power supply doesn't deliver solid 5V, and maybe provides too much power, the board can easily get fried.

Great third-party vendors who can provide your Pi with adequate power are:

- AdaFruit
- MoodMyPi
- SparkFun

SD Card. Its small and its super powerful, but the Raspberry Pi does not have the capability to store data onboard. That is why, and SD (Secure Digital) Card – a removable storage device – is essential.

Here is what you need to look for when shopping for an SD card for your Raspberry Pi:

- A Standard SD Card. Your Pi supports a standard SD card, not a Mini or a Micro SD, however, you can use an adapter to convert these if you happen to have a Micro or Mini.

- A trustworthy brand. Avoid the cheap choices and choose good quality SD card such as Kingston, SanDisk or Transcend.

- At least 4 GB of capacity

- Class 4 or higher. The class is important because it indicates how quickly the card can actually write and read data. For instance, an SD card of class 4 can read and write MB per second. Class 6 is faster with 6 MB per second, class 10 can read 10 MB per second, etc.

Keep in mind that the Standard SD card comes in SDHC (Secure Digital High Capacity) and SDXC (Secure Digital eXtended Capacity). Make sure to check your Pi's compatibility and see which one is best for your device. The SDHC goes up to 32 GB, and the SDXC up to 2T.

Powered USB Hub. An USB hub is a compact device that can host a couple of USB devices. For instance, if you have the low-cost Raspberry Pi, you may have only one or two ports. Plug your mouse and keyboard and you have no way to plug anything else. That is why an USB hub is one of the main things that Raspberry Pi owners buy right after purchasing their tiny computer.

Ethernet Cable. If you want to connect your Raspberry Pi to the Internet (and of course you do), then, besides the obvious Internet connectivity, you will need an Ethernet cable to do so. You plug one end of the Ethernet cable in your Pi and the other in your Wireless router, cable modem, or whatever device you have for connecting to the internet.

Monitor. Even if you plan on using your Raspberry PI heedlessly and remotely, chances are that sooner rather than later, you'll want to plug your computer into a monitor or a TV.

Cables. To plug your Raspberry Pi into a monitor or TV, you will need cables. For this purpose, you will probably need an HDMI cable or a composite video cable.

In case you will be using analog video, you will also need a 3.5 mm stereo audio cable whether you want to get a sound after connecting it to your TV or monitor, or plan on connecting it to external speakers.

USB Mouse and Keyboard. As a computer, the Raspberry Pi also requires a keyboard and a mouse. You can use both wired and wireless, however, know that many users have reported some issues with the wireless keyboards and mice, as most Pi models require that you unplug and plug back in, when the Pi reboots.

Conclusion

Thank you for making it to the end of **Raspberry Pi Beginners Guide: The Ultimate Raspberry Pi 4 Setup, Programming, Projects Guide for Beginners**, remember the Raspberry Pi is commonly used for real-time image/video processing, robotics applications, and IoT based applications. The Raspberry Pi Foundation are the ones that offered the Debian based Raspbian OS. They also provide NOOBS OS for the Raspberry Pi. The Raspbian OS is the official operating system for the Raspberry Pi. It comes with GUI that features tools for Python programming, browsing, office games, and more.

We looked at what this device is all about and some of the benefits that we can enjoy when we use this device for programming, and we even looked at how to get it connected to some of the other parts that you need, such as USB drives, Wi-Fi, and more so that we are able to actually create some of the projects that we want.

In addition, we took a look at some of the different programming things that we need to keep in mind when we go through this process. Obviously, you can't paint a landscape without learning its basics. And the fact that you've read the entire book means that you're really interested in Raspberry Pi. Otherwise, if you were not, you wouldn't have read all the pages. Now, this is only the first step. Remember, you want to be a top-notch Raspberry programmer.

Top-notch programmers don't give up along the way. Go ahead and practice to conceptualize all the ideas you have learned in this book. Remember, the rule of thumb in learning - Raspberry Pi included - is practice; and undoubtedly: Good practice makes perfect.

Every Raspberry Pi model comes with one common thing: they're compatible; indicating software that's built for one model will run on other models as well. This means that it can run the latest version of the Raspberry Pi's operating system on an original prelaunch version, such as the Model B prototype. Though it would run slowly, it will run, nonetheless.

The Raspberry Pi is indeed a technological marvel, and it will always be amazing as to what this tiny machine is capable of. Not only does this little monster pack a punch in terms of power and capability, but the Raspberry Pi is also in a league of its own with regards to its adaptability to an entire array of possible applications. Just as how the Raspberry Pi's usefulness knows no limits and has no defined boundary, we could only learn so much in this beginner's level book. There's still an entire island's worth of knowledge to still explore regarding the Pi and its capability and how we can use it to the best of its abilities. However, this book has addressed all of the essential concepts to their basic form so that the reader will be able to tackle any problem he comes across if he wants to use the Raspberry Pi as a pocket computer or as a project piece.

In short, the Raspberry Pi is a small circuit board capable of big things. Learning about it requires proper guidance, and so far, we have addressed that job to the best of our abilities.

www.ingramcontent.com/pod-product-compliance
Lightning Source LLC
Chambersburg PA
CBHW071138050326
40690CB00008B/1500